Original title:
Threads of Light

Copyright © 2025 Creative Arts Management OÜ
All rights reserved.

Author: Wyatt Kensington
ISBN HARDBACK: 978-1-80586-203-1
ISBN PAPERBACK: 978-1-80586-675-6

Whispers of Tomorrow

In the morning sun, we skip and dance,
Chasing shadows that wear a funny stance.
Socks on our hands and hats on our feet,
Life is a circus—oh, isn't it neat?

With giggles and snorts, we paint the sky,
Colors of dreams, just you and I.
A banana car zooms, a pickle parade,
Juggling our worries, they fade like a shade.

In a world of giggles, we twist and twirl,
Hiccups and laughter make my hair curl.
We sip lemonade from a flower pot,
Planting our joys in a big parking lot.

So let's wear these smiles, let the world see,
How silly and happy our spirits can be.
With a wink and a nudge, we'll break every rule,
Tomorrow's our canvas, just look at the fool!

Sunlit Vibrations

When sunbeams dance on silly hats,
A rooster struts like he's with the bats.
The garden gnomes add to the cheer,
While squirrels plot to steal our beer.

The daisies giggle, they can't hold still,
As bees play tag around the mill.
A flip-flop flops, a dog lets out a bark,
Life's a circus, let's embrace the spark!

Veils of Serenity

A cat in shades lounges on the fence,
While yoga poses seem rather dense.
A breeze whispers secrets to the trees,
As squirrels tie knots in a light summer breeze.

Flip-flops flapping, they're on the scene,
With lemonade laughter, it's quite the routine.
A sandwich flies, is it on a quest?
Whatever it is, we're surely blessed.

Woven Dreams

Sleepy clouds weave hats for the sheep,
As dreams take flight not bound to sleep.
A chicken wears glasses, calls out a tune,
While ducks in a row sneak off to the moon.

The stars in pajamas play hide and seek,
While giggles erupt from the moon's little peak.
We sway on hammocks with giggly delight,
In a world where humor takes glorious flight.

Glimmers in the Dawn

The rooster crows in a glittery coat,
While a duck serenades a sleepy goat.
Sunshine tickles the grass like a tease,
As laughter erupts in the morning breeze.

Pancakes flip as they join a parade,
With syrup rivers that sweetly cascade.
The dawn smiles wide, it's a merry affair,
Where joy is the fabric we all love to wear.

Resonance of Hope

In a world where giggles play,
And silly socks hold sway,
Laughter weaves a crazed delight,
Chasing shadows out of sight.

Bubbles dance like tiny sprites,
In mismatched shoes, there are no fights,
Hope spins round in silly hats,
As joy flies high with acrobats.

The Fabric of the Universe

In a cosmic quilt of hues,
Where even stars wear funny shoes,
Wobbly planets do their dance,
While comets take a goofy chance.

Aliens weave with lots of flair,
They're stitching jokes with cosmic air,
A belt of giggles, bright and bold,
Tales of laughter, new and old.

Lightspun Dreams

In dreams where marshmallows glow,
And donuts sprout a brilliant show,
Silly wishes float and swirl,
As giggles tune the night, they twirl.

Dancing shadows skip and hop,
In pajama pants, they never stop,
A confetti storm of pure delight,
Fills the air with dreams so light.

A Chronicle of Glimmers

Once upon a time in flights,
Glimmers wore the silliest tights,
They twinkled with a raucous cheer,
Spreading giggles ear to ear.

Each sparkle told a cheeky tale,
Of whoopee cushions and a snail,
At twilight's call, they did unite,
To share the joy, the laughs, the light.

Illuminated Journeys

In a world where socks dance free,
A cat wears shades, and that's the key!
The fridge hums tunes of ancient lore,
    Unlocking snacks behind a door.

A squirrel in a hat sings karaoke,
While the toaster pops toast in a strange smoky.
We ride on clouds made of cotton candy,
    Sipping bubbles while feeling dandy.

Celestial Weavings

The moon's in pajamas, what a sight!
Winking at stars, it's quite a night.
The planets play hopscotch in the dark,
While comets chase dreams with a spark.

A nebula of noodles swirls and bends,
As the universe giggles, making amends.
Galaxies twist like spaghetti strands,
Twirling tales from far-off lands.

Dappled Serendipity

The daisies wear hats, polka dot and bright,
Chasing the butterflies, what a delight!
A hedgehog in glasses reads funny books,
While the sun beams down with its warm, cheeky looks.

Lollipops tumble from trees like rain,
And lemonade rivers babble with gain.
Life's quirky dances, we do twirl and twine,
Finding joy in each twist, it's simply divine!

The Dance of Sunbeams

Sunbeams play hide and seek with the wind,
  Tickling the trees where giggles begin.
  They leap on puddles, splash with glee,
    Drawing rainbows, oh what a spree!

A giraffe in flip-flops juggles with flair,
  As bumblebees buzz without a care.
  Kites fly off, in laughter's embrace,
  In this wacky, wonderful, sunny space!

Twilight Tapestry

In twilight's whimsy, colors collide,
The moon wearing glasses, with pride.
Stars giggle softly, pulling their strings,
Juggling their glow, oh the joy it brings!

A bat in a bowtie, dancing with flair,
Twist and turn, without a care.
Fireflies buzzing like little tailors,
Stitching the night with sparkly trailers!

The Dance of Daybreak

Morning embodies a playful tease,
Sun in pajamas, brewing with ease.
Waking the world with a tickle and stretch,
Even the roosters forgot how to fetch!

Clouds wearing hats as they drift along,
Listening closely for day's silly song.
The sun throws confetti, bright and bold,
Chasing the shadows, break out of their mold!

Glowing Threads of Life

Nature's puppets pull silly pranks,
Squirrels in tutus, waving their flanks.
Chasing each other in a bright-eyed spree,
Even the flowers join in with glee!

Bubbles of laughter float up in the air,
Bee in a bowler, without a care.
Butterflies giggle, not afraid to roam,
In gardens of whimsy, they always feel home!

Vignettes of Light

Laughter flickers in the evening's hue,
Fireflies waltzing, a party for two.
Crickets reciting their nighttime shows,
Amidst the chuckles, the moon softly glows!

Candles competing in a flickering race,
Knocking over matches, oh what a place!
Silliness sprouts in the gloaming delight,
As shadows play tag, giving hearts a light!

Dawn's Gentle Brush

When the sun yawns wide and bright,
Cats stretch out, claiming their right.
Coffee cups tremble with glee,
As toast does a wiggly dance, so free.

Waking up is quite an art,
With socks that never find their part.
Pajamas provide the perfect flair,
As I hop around looking everywhere.

Silk and Sparks

In the closet, a dress does prance,
It screams, "Put me on for a chance!"
Breezy skirts flirt with the wind,
As mismatched shoes twirl and spin.

My hairbrush fights a tangled war,
While a rogue sock rolls out to score.
It's a fashion show gone absurd,
Where style is the loudest word.

Beneath the Radiant Veil

At the park, shadows play peek-a-boo,
While squirrels debate the best nut stew.
Bees buzz jokes in a busy line,
While grass tickles toes, oh so divine.

Wiggly worms have a dance-off spree,
As mad hats hop with glee.
A picnic unfolds with clumsy flair,
With ants attending, but unaware.

Dance of the Fireflies

Fireflies put on their sparkly coats,
With tiny shoes and lightweight floats.
They jig and jive in a glowing spree,
While frogs give rhythm, as cross as can be.

Twilight giggles at their little show,
With moths trying hard not to be slow.
The night is alive with a luminous grin,
As bugs bust moves, where do I begin?

Glimmers in the Gloom

In the dark, we all trip,
On shoelaces of glow, what a flip!
The fridge light is a beacon,
Guiding snacks in the need for a whip.

A cat knocks down a lamp,
It shines bright, what a champ!
Dancing shadows on the wall,
Life's like a quirky old stamp.

Mops with sparkles, oh so bright,
Swirling dust twirls in delight.
We laugh at the broom's little dance,
In the oddness, everything's right.

So here's to the silliness found,
Where giggles and glitters abound.
When life gives you dark, crack a joke,
And let your own laughter resound.

Twined Aureate Whispers

Golden threads in grandma's yarn,
Kittens play, oh the charm!
Weaves of mischief on the floor,
As I trip, I can't stay calm.

A squirrel steals a shiny ring,
Off to show the tree bling!
The sun winks through clouds above,
Nature's own little fling.

Make a crown of dandelions,
With bees buzzing like violins.
I wear it, feeling like a queen,
While ants march like they're in spin.

With laughter woven in the air,
And moments that spiral with flair.
These tiny joys, golden and bright,
Make each moment rare.

Chasing Celestial Streaks

In a yard full of fireflies,
I chase them like pie in the skies.
My brother claims he's a wizard,
But it's just Dad's old ties!

Comets made of shoe laces,
Zooming with all their graces.
We twirl under a blanket of stars,
While the dog plays in odd places.

With dreams soaring over the fence,
And laughter that's simply immense.
The night stroll feels like a race,
Who knew gnomes had such suspense?

So grab a friend and take a ride,
On adventures where laughter collides.
We'll map the milky way of fun,
As silly dreams take us on strides.

Filaments of Hope

A squirrel's stash of acorn delight,
Reminds me to save for the night.
When the fridge is empty and bare,
Every crumb feels like a bite!

The vacuum hums a jolly tune,
Chasing dust bunnies around the room.
With every peek I'm on a quest,
For joy hides in the smallest gloom.

Banana peels slip, whoops, whoa,
I laugh at my tripping, oh no!
Even mishaps dance in the light,
Making life a funny show.

So here's to the stray bits of cheer,
That spiral and twirl, oh dear!
With every blunder comes a grin,
And laughter is what we hold dear.

Woven Radiance

In a loom made of giggles, they weave with flair,
Knitting sunbeams and laughter, as if they don't care.
Each loop is a chuckle, each stitch a loud roar,
Creating a fabric that begs you for more.

A cat in a sunbeam, lounging with glee,
Purring like a machine, a soft melody.
It's all in the fibers, the warmth of the fun,
Chasing shadows with antics, until the day's done.

Luminous Pathways

Dancing on sidewalks made of bright jellybeans,
Shiny shoes squeaking, bursting at the seams.
Step on a bubble, it pops with a cheer,
Follow the giggles; they're music to hear.

Silly silhouettes under a glowing disco ball,
Strutting and spinning, without any fall.
Twinkling like fireflies, they trip and they slide,
In this carnival chaos, joy is the guide.

Shimmering Echoes

In the valley of chuckles where echoes abound,
Laughter ricochets; it's the best kind of sound.
A parrot in bow-ties gives everyone sass,
His jokes are so clever, they make the time pass.

Sipping on drizzle from a sparkling cup,
How do you drink joy? You just fill it up!
Beneath the giggling stars, the shadows will play,
As the night spins in circles, a humorous ballet.

Tapestry of Dawn

When morning breaks in with a rumble and grin,
Socks mismatched on feet, let the fun begin!
Each sunbeam a noodle that twists and it twirls,
Making breakfast with flair, as the pancake swirls.

Waffles piled high on the plate like a throne,
With syrupy rivers that shimmer and moan.
A parade of giggles marches out of the door,
In this tapestry woven, there's always room for more.

Radiant Connections

In the attic, the bulbs pop,
Flickering like a bouncy top.
Every glow is a merry cheer,
As the cat starts to disappear.

Laughter spills from every wall,
Echoing like a bouncing ball.
Those lights dance without a care,
Saying, 'Join us, if you dare!'

The toaster winks with a bright grin,
Its toast is always crisp within.
While the fridge hums a jolly tune,
Inviting you for a late-night swoon.

So gather 'round this shining crew,
Where the silly bulbs spark joy anew.
In this chaos, find your delight,
And chase the shadows with pure light!

Veins of Brilliance

A lightbulb fell, but did it shatter?
No, it bounced off like a happy patter.
With a flick and a twist, it glows,
Hoping to shine like a garden hose.

In the kitchen, pots are gleaming,
Their reflections bright and screaming.
Every spoon has a tale to tell,
Of dinners cooked that rang the bell.

A disco ball in the living room,
Swirling shadows begins to loom.
The dog starts to dance, what a sight,
As we laugh at this goofy plight!

So grab your friends, and join the spree,
Where laughter flows so light and free.
With sparkles bouncing off the floor,
Who needs sunlight anymore?

Ethereal Strands

The fairy lights twinkle with glee,
An ecstatic party of jubilee.
Each glimmer seems to have a joke,
Even the cactus bursts out in smoke.

Banana peels left on the floor,
Get tangled with lights, oh what a score!
While the hamster spins in delight,
As we dance into the starry night.

Ghostly figures from the past,
Join in the fun, but they can't last.
With every flash, they start to sway,
Cackling, 'We love this wild display!'

So let's raise a toast to this odd sight,
Where shadows prance and spirits light.
In laughter's embrace, we'll stay awhile,
With dreams as silly as a rubbery smile!

A Tangle of Emotions

Oh, the joys of tangled wires,
A circus act of our desires.
With each connection, sparks might fly,
But don't worry, we'll just laugh and cry.

Lamps winking like they're in on fun,
Why's the toaster always on the run?
It pops up bags of laughs galore,
As we roll around and hit the floor.

Juggling feelings like a clown,
Though some days we might feel down.
But with each giggle and bright prank,
We find joy in the mess we make.

So let's embrace this crazy ride,
With tangled threads by our side.
In this carnival of silly sights,
We dance through scrambled days and nights!

Crystalline Echoes

In a world of glitter, I lost my shoe,
Dancing with shadows, what else could I do?
My cat pulled my socks, they flew in a spree,
Laughing at chaos, oh what a sight to see!

Glimmers of mischief sparkle and shine,
A rabbit in glasses, sipping on brine.
Who knew that the sun could giggle or tease?
Twirling with stars, I'm brought to my knees!

Why is my sandwich wearing a hat?
It whispers to me, "Who's daft enough for that?"
With jelly and cream, it dances on bread,
A culinary circus inside my head!

Each bump in the road is a bouncy parade,
With pickles as confetti, it's simply well-played.
So let's twirl in the ruckus, embrace all the fun,
For life is a waltz that's just come undone!

Shimmering Horizons

Oh, the moon wears pajamas, don't you agree?
Twinkling and laughing, as bright as can be.
A star caught my eye, it winks with a grin,
Said, "Get ready for jokes, let the fun begin!"

The sun in the morning, a jester on stage,
Bouncing on beams, it bursts from the cage.
Tickling the clouds with a tag and a tease,
A comedy show that will never cease!

My goldfish recites Shakespeare each night,
With bubbles and flair, it's a curious sight.
While frogs hold a dance that defies every law,
"Ribbit, ribbit, come see, we're redefining awe!"

Not one day is normal under this sky,
With whimsy and wonder, we laugh 'til we cry.
So join in the fun as we skip and we run,
For life's a grand play and we're all here for fun!

Light's Embrace

Balloons in the wind, they chaotically spin,
Kite-flying lessons from a cheeky old kin.
They tango with trees, and giggle with glee,
Who knew that a breeze could be such a spree?

A squirrel with style dons a tiny beret,
Strolling through shadows, it's here for the play.
Nuts in its pockets, it's ready to burst,
With every fine nibble, our laughter is cursed!

When daylight gives way to the night's cosmic cheer,
Fireflies pop out, with their glow and their sneer.
"Catch us if you can!" they swoosh and they glide,
A chase that ignites, let the humor be wide!

So raise up your glasses, let's toast with a cheer,
To mischief, mayhem, and moments so dear.
For together we dance under each little spark,
In a world of delight, let our joy leave a mark!

A Fabric of Brilliance

A patchwork of giggles, a tapestry bright,
Stitches of laughter sewn with pure light.
In the kitchen, the blender's a DJ with flair,
Dancing with veggies, oh, what a square!

Behold the odd socks in a brilliant parade,
They waltz through the laundry, so neatly displayed.
With polka dots swirling, and stripes on the run,
A fashion faux pas turned whimsical fun!

In the garden, the sunflowers try to outshine,
Competing with daisies in a floral divine.
With petals like smiles, all twinkling and bright,
They whisper to bees, "Let's buzz through the night!"

So gather your giggles and let laughter reign,
With stories and snickers that dance in the rain.
Our world's stitched together with whimsical glee,
In this fabric of brilliance, let's all just be free!

Radiant Horizons

A chicken crossed the road, so bright,
To catch the rays in golden light.
She clucked in glee, her beak aglow,
Singing songs to the sun below.

With shades upon her feathery head,
She danced with joy, laughing instead.
The other birds all rolled their eyes,
At this odd sight, a true surprise.

The sun winked down, a playful spark,
As the chicken strutted, made her mark.
"Why did you cross?" a duckling asked,
"To bask in fun! It's all I've tasked!"

So every dawn, she'll take a stand,
In a sunny show, a quirky band.
And though the world may scratch its head,
She shines her light, and laughs instead.

Echoing Splendor

A parrot told a knock-knock joke,
It echoed loud, the forest spoke.
The trees all giggled, swayed in glee,
As the parrot danced on a tall, green tree.

A squirrel shouted, "Who's there?" with flair,
The punchline landed in the air.
A laughter fit, it ricocheted,
As daisies chuckled, brightly swayed.

Bees buzzed in rhythm, joining the chat,
While the grass below wore a smiley hat.
Nature's comedy, in every nook,
A circus of joy, all in one book.

The moon peeked in, a glowing shade,
As they shared more jokes, unafraid.
In a world so green and never bland,
Laughter echoed, every moment planned.

Embered Tides

The waves came in with a splat and a splash,
Crabs dancing funny, making a dash.
While seashells giggled, in glittering pools,
Jellyfish wobbled, defying the rules.

A seagull squawked in a raspy tune,
Joking with fish in the afternoon.
A surfboard hopped, lost at sea,
While a starfish laughed, "That's just like me!"

The sun, it chuckled as it sank low,
Turning the ocean a shimmering glow.
With every ripple, the humor spread,
Beneath a sky where the laughter led.

So as twilight falls and the tide retreats,
Ocean's giggles mix with heartbeats.
In this great expanse, where fun resides,
Life's a tide of laughter, in joyous rides.

Twilight's Caress

In a garden where the shadows play,
A cat in a hat had something to say.
"Do you know why the moon is round?"
"To catch all the dreams that are lost and found!"

With flowers laughing in shades so bright,
They whispered secrets on this fine night.
A mouse in slippers waved quite grand,
"I throw the best parties in this land!"

The fireflies flickered, a disco ball,
As nature's creatures began their call.
"Let's dance until the stars fall down!"
Cried a ladybug in a tiny crown.

So twilight wraps them in colors bold,
A whimsical night, stories retold.
In laughter and joy, their hearts confess,
That life's a tease, in its sweet caress.

Dreaming in Color

In a world where socks collide,
And dance their pairs away,
A sock hops on one foot,
Mismatched in bright ballet.

The sun wears shades of neon,
While clouds play hide-and-seek,
A rainbow paints a picture,
Of silliness at its peak.

Bouncing like a jellybean,
Colors pop and spin,
As giggles fill the air,
And joy begins to win.

In this canvas of the silly,
Dreams are hues so bold,
With laughter and with brightness,
A story to be told.

Fabric of the Cosmos

In a suit made out of stardust,
A comet wears a tie,
While planets roll like marbles,
And asteroids drift by.

A galactic grandma knits,
With yarn spun from the sun,
She crochets black hole potholders,
Her cosmic work is fun!

Nebulas do a conga,
In colors wild and bright,
Twinkling stars clap their hands,
Underneath the moonlight.

While meteors race through space,
They giggle in a race,
For in this silly fabric,
Everything finds its place.

Radiant Mosaics

A patchwork quilt of laughter,
Stitched by giggling seams,
Where kittens wear pajamas,
In the world of vivid dreams.

Butterflies don top hats,
With polka dots and flair,
While carrots play the trumpet,
In the sunlit, funny air.

This jigsaw of bright moments,
Creates a masterpiece,
Where jellybeans are waiters,
And humor won't cease.

So let's embrace the color,
And all the joy it brings,
Life's crazy radiant mosaic,
Where laughter always sings.

Light's Dance Upon the Water

The river giggles softly,
As ducks wear silly hats,
They waddle to the rhythm,
And do a little dance.

A fish jumps like a dancer,
With sparkles in its wake,
While frogs leap with glee,
For fun is what they make.

The sunlight joins the party,
While ripples laugh and sway,
Together they create,
A splashy cabaret.

So let's all dip our toes,
In this whimsical affair,
For life is but a dance,
And joy is everywhere.

Celestial Weavings

In the sky where giggles bloom,
Starry socks hang with no room.
Comets chase their tails in haste,
While moonlight spills, like soup, unbraced.

Planets dance in polka dots,
Jupiter's slipping on his knots.
Saturn spins with rings so broad,
They're just a hula hoop gone odd.

Asteroids play hide and seek,
But they always bump their cheeks.
By the sun, a joke is told,
As solar winds blow out the cold.

In this space where laughter gleams,
Cosmic dreams are wacky schemes.
Hitch a ride on a comet's tail,
And tell the stars a funny tale.

Veils of Glimmer

A veil of sparkles flutters bright,
Fairies laugh at their own flight.
One's tripped on a daisy's cap,
Sending sprinkles in a flap.

Glimmer's got a silly grin,
As giggles dance, it starts to spin.
Where every shimmer's lost its way,
And moonbeams play all night and day.

The light jests, teasing shadows near,
"Catch me if you can, my dear!"
But shadows only stomp their feet,
And trip on laughter, oh so sweet.

In this magic chaos grows,
Where fun unfolds and mischief flows.
And as the veil starts to unveil,
Laughter reigns; we shall prevail!

Brilliance Unraveled

A tangle of sparkles, what a mess!
Twinkling lights, like a wild dress.
They pop and fizz with silly glee,
In a dance that shouts, "Look at me!"

The sun wears shades, all hip and cool,
While the stars gather for a pool.
They splash and laugh, a cosmic cheer,
It's the brightest party of the year!

Light bulbs buzz with zap and zing,
As laughter bounces, oh what a swing!
Chasing rainbows with paintbrush wits,
Making jokes with sparkly hits.

In this chaos where colors blend,
Each giggle seems to have a friend.
Unraveled shimmer, tangled fate,
A radiant laugh we celebrate!

Splintered Sunlight

Splinters dance with colors bright,
Sunbeams giggle, what a sight!
They bounce about, in quirky ways,
Tickling clouds on sunny days.

A flash! A dash! Splatters flair,
As sunlight plays without a care.
With every twist, a silly wink,
Making puddles laugh and blink.

In the evening, beams misbehave,
Shadow puppets try to wave.
But sunlit giggles steal the show,
A bright embrace of radiant glow.

Splintered laughter fills the air,
As sunlight casts its playful snare.
In this whimsical, silly flight,
We find our joy within the light.

Beams of Serenity

In the morning, cats stretch long,
While coffee spills, oh so wrong.
The toast pops up, flies like a bird,
And I just chuckle, haven't you heard?

A squirrel jumps, on a bright parade,
Chasing its tail, a mad charade.
A sunbeam dances, across my floor,
As I trip over shoes, what a chore!

The clock ticks loudly, a silly tune,
While I sing to the dish, morning's boon.
Bananas in pajamas, peeking through,
It's a circus here, what else is new?

With smiles so wide, laughter unfolds,
In this silly life, where joy foretold.
So raise your cup, cheerfully clink,
In a world of giggles, stop to think.

Flickering Flames of Dawn

The sun rolls in, but oh dear me,
A sock on the cat? What a sight to see!
My cereal's swimming, milk like a sea,
Eating breakfast's turning into a spree!

A pillow fight breaks out with a laugh,
Dancing on corpses of breakfast's aftermath.
The clock's winking at me, saying 'You're late,'
While pancakes wave goodbye on my plate!

The door swings wide, and I trip in style,
With dancing shoes that clearly beguile.
Umbrellas swirling in an odd ballet,
As I skip outside, running away.

Strange the ways, a new day can start,
With laughter and folly, oh what a part!
In the flicker of dawn, where giggles ignite,
Life feels like a joke, oh what a delight!

Chasing Sunbeams

Chasing shadows, we run so fast,
But oops, fell into the dog's last cast!
Giggles erupt as we race the breeze,
With candy in pockets, oh how to tease!

We spot a butterfly, its colors bright,
But it flutters away like it's taking flight.
"Catch it!" I yell, as we dash and weave,
Until we trip over, all we can grieve!

Sunbeams glitter, like confetti in air,
With laughter and joy, without a care.
A hopscotch game, drawn quick with a stick,
Each jump brings laughter, even if it's thick!

At day's end, we lay down our heads,
With giggling dreams, slipping under beds.
In chasing the light, we find our fun,
With dappled sunshine, the day is done.

Illuminated Journeys

Packing my bags, it's time to roam,
With mismatched socks, calling it home.
A map upside down, oh what a sight,
We're lost in laughter, but feeling all right!

The car's making noises, a tune of its own,
As we swerve through the trees, like we've flown.
With snacks galore, crammed in the back,
An epic road trip? Oh, it's off track!

We stop for ice cream, it's melting fast,
Dropping flavors, what a sticky blast!
Silly selfies with cones in hand,
Life's just a giggle in this strange land!

With sunsets painted, like a kid's wild art,
Adventures we share, straight from the heart.
Thank you for joining my wacky quest,
In journeys so bright, we are truly blessed!

Sunbeams in the Mist

In foggy mornings where shadows play,
Sunbeams giggle in a cheeky way.
They chase the clouds, give them a shove,
Like playful pups, they dance and shove.

With coffee cups held high in glee,
They tickle noses, wild and free.
But just when you think you've caught a ray,
It slips away, and shouts, 'Not today!'

The squirrels giggle, oh what a sight,
Chasing beams in a morning light.
One jumped high, slipped on a leaf,
Landed in mud, what a comical grief!

So when you wake with a silly grin,
Remember the beams where the laugh begins.
In misty mornings, let's take our flight,
Chasing the giggles, oh what delight!

The Glow Between Moments

Between each tick of the old clock's chime,
Lies a glow that dances, oh so sublime.
Like awkward uncles at a wedding's feast,
Its fizzy laughter never seems to cease.

It peeks from behind the cereal box,
And winks from socks that resemble rocks.
You might trip over a playful spark,
That lights the hallways—a funny quirk!

With each little giggle, the daylight breathes,
Stirring up bubbles, and swaying leaves.
One misstep, and you're in quite the hoot,
As shiny beams chase your worn-out boot!

So embrace the glow in these quirky days,
And dance through life in whimsical ways.
For the laughter that lives in those fleeting flashes,
Is the magic that lingers and never crashes!

Chasing Radiance

In fields where daisies bloom and sway,
Bright sparks chase butterflies, frolic and play.
They leap and twirl with a twinkling laugh,
Building castles of light on a sunny path.

They hide behind trees with a cheeky grin,
Just when you look, they vanish again.
But catch one quick—oh don't be slow,
It tickles your ear like a ticklish glow!

The laughter erupts as they shine and spin,
Like a wacky race, let the fun begin!
In a world where giggles spark the air,
The chase for brightness is truly rare.

So gather your friends and run wild and free,
Join the sunlight in its whimsical spree.
For in every chase, an adventure ignites,
And you'll find joy in the playful lights!

Luminous Pathways

Along the winding roads of glee,
Luminous paths beckon you and me.
With every step, they break into song,
A silly jig where we all belong.

They spill like jelly down the parkway,
And dance like clowns in a bright, silly sway.
Just watch your step, or you'll slip and slide,
Into a puddle, let the laughter ride!

With every giggle, the shadows retreat,
As light strolls through, tapping its feet.
A parade of colors brightens the scene,
Like exuberant kids in a candy dream!

So twirl with the glow, and bask in the mirth,
For laughter, my friend, is a gift of great worth.
On luminous pathways, let silliness reign,
In this joyous journey, we all gain!

Incandescent Echoes

In a world where bulbs dance and twirl,
Glowing so bright, they create a whirl.
A light bulb's laugh, a flickering cheer,
Echoes of joy, that everyone hears.

The lanterns chuckle in the summer night,
Bugs in tuxedos, oh what a sight!
They sip on nectar, like it's champagne,
Under the stars, they feel no pain.

A candle's wink, a flash of glee,
Who knew wax had such a degree?
In this bright circus, laughter ignites,
The glow of good humor, a true delight!

So when you find yourself feeling low,
Just look for the glow, let your laughter flow.
For in this bright world, absurdity reigns,
With incandescent echoes, joy remains.

A Symphony of Glow

In the daylight, sun plays a tune,
With rays that dance, from morning to noon.
But when night falls, and stars appear,
The moon joins in, and the world must cheer!

A neon sign humming a cheeky refrain,
Bats in sunglasses, are totally insane.
They flit and they flutter, doing their thing,
While disco balls make the shadows swing!

The candles wiggle, as if they could sing,
While lightbulbs wobble, in a silly ring.
Together they make a joyous parade,
In this radiant concert, there's no charade.

So grab a partner, and join the show,
Dance with the rays, let your worries go.
In this symphony, laughter is found,
With a chorus of glow, oh what a sound!

Colors of the Dawn

As dawn breaks, colors spill wide,
Like spilled jellybeans, in a sugar slide.
The orange giggles, yellow does waltz,
While pink whispers softly, no fault at all!

Clouds dress up in their whimsical best,
With shades so vibrant, they put smiles to the test.
Lavender chuckles as it drifts along,
A watercolor dream, where all belong!

A sunbeam races with a gleeful shout,
Tickling flowers, causing a pout.
While children giggle, catching the hues,
In this splendid game, there's nothing to lose!

So rise with the colors, dance and play,
In the silly sunrise, let worries drift away.
A morning so cheery, there's beauty in fun,
With colors of joy, shining like the sun!

Lights Among Shadows

In corners where shadows like to creep,
Lights pop up, making mischief deep.
A flashlight game, tag, it's on!
With giggles and whispers, the fun's never gone!

The streetlamp winks, a sly little sprite,
Waving hello to the dogs in flight.
While shadows pretend to play hide and seek,
Those sneaky, sneaky figures, not a word do they speak!

A glow from below, what could it be?
A glow worm party, come dance with me!
They twirl and they jiggle, glimmering bright,
Casting silly shapes in the moon's soft light.

So embrace the glow, let laughter resound,
In a world where even shadows get unbound.
With lights all around, let humor ignite,
In the playful twilight, everything feels right!

Flickers of the Beyond

In the night, stars play hide and seek,
Twinkling like they've had too much to drink.
A comet zooms, with a tail so bright,
It trips on shadows; what a silly sight!

Moonbeams bounce on my cat's little nose,
She chases them like a dog with a hose.
Dancing on rooftops, the fairies cheer,
Telling the moon to keep the light near.

From Jupiter's rings to Saturn's flair,
Aliens chuckle, hanging out in midair.
They drop some giggles and a wink or two,
While playing hopscotch in the cosmic blue.

When the sun yawns, it stretches wide,
Waking up planets, giving stars a ride.
Galaxies whirl in a cosmic jive,
As laughter echoes, keeping dreams alive.

Vibrations of the Cosmos

In the cosmos, laughter swirls and twirls,
Asteroids giggle, with bright little curls.
The sun cracks jokes, shining so bold,
While the planets shriek, 'We're not that old!'

Shooting stars sing, oh what a tune,
Making wishes by the light of the moon.
Alien parties rock on moons made of cheese,
With dancing space cows, swaying with ease.

Nebulas puff like popcorn in air,
Creating shapes, a true cosmic fair.
Spirals of whispers float like balloons,
Bouncing off comets, singing sweet tunes.

As black holes yawn, they pull guests in,
But they leave the jokes; oh what a sin!
Under a starry giggle-fest, we sway,
Making trouble in the milky way.

Light-Cast Patterns

Patterns flicker on the wall tonight,
A dance of shadows in the pale moonlight.
Cupcake stars with frosting so fine,
Sway with the winds, in a cosmic line.

A toaster pops while planets revolve,
Spitting out bread like it's trying to solve.
Sunlight snickers as it fills the room,
Casting jokes that make flowers bloom.

Rainbows giggle, sliding down a slide,
Splashes of color, in joy abide.
Jellybeans rolling across the floor,
Playing tag with the light from the door.

With every flicker, a joke appears,
Whispering laughter across the spheres.
So let's embrace this silly delight,
As the day unfurls with giggles of light.

Luminous Threads of Fate

Bright ribbons dance in the cosmic air,
Tying up mischief with a twinkle and flare.
An octopus juggles, a sight to behold,
Sparking confetti as it twirls and unfolds.

Smart stars wear glasses, looking for fun,
Binge-watching galaxies, oh what a run!
Meteor showers rain down some cheer,
With jokes so bright, they're hard to steer!

The sun spills lemonade, in a cosmic cup,
While planets sip quietly and erupt.
Giggles from galaxies scattered afar,
Make space a playground, like a shooting star.

Every moment laughs, in the vast expanse,
Fate spins in circles, inviting a dance.
So let's join in, with our silly parade,
In this luminous map, let's not be afraid.

The Weavings of Time

In a world of tangled yarn,
I spun a tale quite bizarre.
My cat joined in the fray,
Now he's wearing a scarf from my stay.

My sandwiches dance a jig,
As the toaster sings a gig.
I lost my shoes in the bake,
But the bread loaves make no mistake!

The clock ticked backwards today,
As I watched my socks sway.
A penguin waltzed by with flair,
Now we share my rather small chair.

As the fabric of time unwinds,
I see noodle shapes of all kinds.
In this patchwork of silly delight,
Reality is just a big kite!

Spectrums of Solitude

In my room of hidden despair,
I found a sock that could dance in the air.
Its partner's off somewhere,
Probably shopping for underwear!

Next to me, a mirror grins,
As I practice my silly spins.
The toothbrush joins with a sigh,
We all make a lovely pot pie!

My thoughts zigzag wildly about,
Like a squirrel that's trying to shout.
In this spectrum, I will sneak,
And wear pajamas for a week!

On solitary days like this,
I find it's chaos I can't miss.
The vacuum cleaner sings so loud,
Together we'll form a merry crowd!

Dappled Glow

A rainbow landed by my feet,
And it smells like something sweet.
I tried to catch it for a snack,
But it slipped right through the crack!

The sunbeams played hide and seek,
With shadows that kissed my cheek.
My garden gnomes had a ball,
They danced until they started to fall.

I painted stars on every wall,
And invited the moon to call.
It shrugged and said, "I'm too bright!"
And left me here, what a sight!

In the dappled glow I reside,
With unicorns that can't quite glide.
They prance and dance in silly ways,
As we laugh through our sunny days!

Shimmering Pathways

A squirrel on a bicycle flies,
Down shimmering paths where laughter lies.
Its helmet sparkles in the sun,
With a kickstand that thinks it's done!

I followed the glow of a starry map,
Only to find a chatting chap.
He said, "Care to share a cookie?"
But it crumbled all over the rookies!

Invisible fairies threw a ball,
That bounced and giggled, quite tall.
I tried to join their frolic spree,
But tripped and fell by a peach tree.

Along these paths where wonders thrive,
I find that silliness is alive.
So let us frolic and have some fun,
For life's a race that's just begun!

The Glow Within

A banana peel slipped, oh what a sight,
My kitchen's a dance floor, it's quite the delight.
With giggles erupting from pots on the stove,
Who knew that my cooking could be such a trove?

The fridge light laughs at the leftovers' fate,
Juggling the ketchup, the mustard, the plate.
In this circus of food, I'm the clown with a grin,
For each meal's a jest when the omelet won't spin.

The cookie jar hides like a treasure chest,
While I plot my escape, oh what a quest!
Just one little nibble, it won't hurt, I swear,
But the crumbs on my shirt show I'm not being fair!

So dance, silly kitchen, with whisk and with pie,
Every whisking creation is reaching for the sky.
In laughter, there's flavor, a magical mix,
While I'm lost in my cooking's hilarious tricks.

Shards of Radiance

A squirrel just called me, oh what a bold tease,
Offering acorns like gourmet cheese.
I laughed so hard, fell right on the grass,
Nature's a comedy, with critters and sass.

The sun peeked out, wearing sunglasses so cool,
With beams on my head, it felt like a jewel.
A butterfly giggled, doing flips in the air,
While I trip on my sandals, how do I fare?

In puddles of laughter, the rain drops a tune,
Dancing on sidewalks, I'm a goofball balloon.
Streetlights wink out like they're in on the joke,
As I dance with the shadows and trip on the cloak.

And as the night falls, with stars shining bright,
I'm spinning around in the glow of delight.
In this crazy old world, with its zany parade,
Laughter's the treasure that never will fade.

The Fabric of Stars

My toaster's a rocket, blasting off toast,
With butter like stardust, I'm dreaming the most.
The pancakes are planets, flipping through space,
As I gather my breakfast with intergalactic grace.

The coffee's a nebula, swirling with flair,
While spoons dance like martians, floating in air.
I sip on the cosmos, it's out of this world,
While visions of syrup like galaxies swirled.

The fridge holds the cosmos, a vacuum of snacks,
Where aliens whisper and perform silly acts.
I wade through the veggies, like swimming in stars,
As carrots and peas giggle, no need for guitars.

So feast on this universe, so bountiful, bright,
Every meal's an adventure, from day into night.
In this grand kitchen cosmos, I've found my own way,
With laughter as stardust, I dance every day.

Glowing Reveries

In pajamas all day, I'm a lounging machine,
With popcorn as my crown, I'm the snack-munching queen.
The couch is my throne, it gives quite the view,
Of sitcoms and bubble baths, all sparkles anew.

The cat is my jester, with wild acrobatics,
Leaping around like he's got magic mechanics.
While I snicker at dreams of glitter and light,
I wish on my chips for a chipmunk to fight.

The remote is a wand, I wield with great pride,
Changing channels, forget all the outside.
My snack bowl's an orb, filled with joy and delight,
As flavors collide in my cozy, fun night.

So here in my kingdom of pillows and snacks,
Each laughter, each crunch is the joy that it lacks.
In dreams slightly silly, where fun never quits,
The glow of good times is where my heart sits.

Celestial Stitches

In the sky, a little seam,
Stars are stitching dreams extreme.
With needles bright, they poke and play,
Making wishes fly away.

Moon's a tailor, just for fun,
Sewing sunshine, one by one.
Twirling comets, fancy flair,
Fashion shows in cosmic air.

Constellation's fashion week,
Shooting stars that brightly streak.
Fuzzy Orion lost his thread,
Now he's wearing thoughts instead!

Look at Pluto, dressed in ice,
Wants to be a star, so nice.
Frolicking in velvet night,
Sewing laughs with pure delight.

Sunlit Shadows

Sunbeams dance on rooftops bright,
Casting shadows left and right.
Joking squirrels in the park,
Making shapes, a silly lark.

Wobbling rabbits hop about,
In the light, they twist and shout.
Juggling nuts in golden rays,
Chasing shadows, joyous plays.

Even trees wear silly grins,
Bending low with playful spins.
Their branches tickle, swish and sway,
While the sun just laughs away.

Watch the shadows start to tease,
Twirling round like autumn breeze.
In the daylight, every sight,
Makes the world a pure delight.

Rays of Promise

Morning comes with golden beams,
Frogs are croaking, sudden dreams.
Promises that jump and shine,
In the puddles, frogs align.

Dandelions, crowns of cheer,
Tickle noses far and near.
Wishing on a fuzzy puff,
Hoping for some silly stuff.

Bees are buzzing, hats askew,
Sipping nectar, how they stew!
Planning parties for the hive,
Bringing joy, they come alive.

Sunset paints a goofy face,
While the stars just take their place.
Each little wink, a wink of jest,
In this day, we are all blessed.

Glowing Connections

Fireflies flicker in a line,
Making sure that all is fine.
With a giggle and a glow,
They link up, a light parade show.

Crickets chirp the tunes that bind,
Joining in, a perfect kind.
By the moon, they dance and sway,
Chasing twinkles on display.

Pixies laugh, a merry crew,
Dancing on the evening dew.
Their laughter echoes, quite a reel,
Bouncing off the night with zeal.

When the stars all start to wink,
In each spark, there's room to think.
Funny moments intertwined,
Glowing hearts, a light designed.

Illuminated Footprints

When stepping out at night with flair,
I spotted glow worms in the air,
They dance upon the path with cheer,
To guide the way, they're always near.

A squirrel in shades, with shades so bright,
Was sipping on a soda, what a sight!
It waved hello, then danced away,
Leaving footprints of glitter, oh what a play!

With twinkling shoes upon my feet,
Each step becomes a funny beat,
Flashes of color, sparks of glee,
Who knew the night would party for me?

A rabbit hops in disco style,
With moonbeams flashing, oh so wild!
We leap and twirl, a merry bunch,
In a world where stars are up for munch!

Halos of Joy

I met a cat with a golden crown,
Strolling through the park, oh, what a clown!
With frolic and purrs, it spread delight,
While wearing sparkling shoes, oh, what a sight!

A dog in boots taps toes to the beat,
Twisting and turning on furry feet,
Each wag a thread of joy that flies,
Under the watchful glow of the skies!

A turtle sporting shades so cool,
Takes a ride on a skateboard, breaking the rule,
The crowd erupts with laughter and cheer,
"Who knew slowpokes could rocket in gear?"

With giggles and wiggles, the night echos back,
In halos of gleeful joy, we all pack,
A whimsical night, each moment we share,
Dancing together without a care.

Pearls of Luminescence

Bubbles in the air like glowing pearls,
Juggling them is easy, watch them twirls,
I slipped on one, flew high in the night,
Landing in a bush, what a silly flight!

A parrot paints the sky with a wink,
While I'm busy pondering, "What do you think?"
It squawks jokes, while tossing confetti,
We laugh till we're dizzy, isn't it petty?

The moon peeked down with a giggly face,
Not making fun, but joining the race,
With glowing stars in a playful dance,
Who knew the night could lead to such chance?

So gather the pearls from the night sky bright,
We'll share silly tales in the pale moonlight,
For moments like these, we can't let them slip,
In this sea of laughter, let's take a dip!

Spun from Stardust

In pajamas made of cosmic fluff,
I tried to fly, but things got tough,
Like a rocket blushing, my face turned red,
The stardust cushions broke my bed!

A fish in a tutu swam by with grace,
Spinning around in the moon's embrace,
"I'm here for the party, want to join in?"
We leaped through the waves, let the fun begin!

With comets throwing sparkles, we pranced,
Each slip and slide left us entranced,
The universe echoed with laughter's song,
"Come join the fun; you can't go wrong!"

So let's twirl with the stars and dance in glee,
In a world of wonders, wild and free,
With every giggle spun from the night,
We are all glowing, under cosmic light!

Flickers of Infinity

A firefly dances, a tiny spark,
A wobbly flight in the dusky dark.
Each flicker a wink, a cosmic tease,
Whispering secrets to swaying trees.

In the vastness of night, they're having a ball,
A party for insects, who could've called?
Juggling with photons, a glimmering show,
If only the moon would join in the glow!

The stars look on with a twinkling grin,
Offering snacks from the light years within.
A buffet of laughter, a dash of delight,
As shadows dance freely, till dawn's first light.

Ethereal Stitches

Needles of moonlight in the midnight sky,
Sewing the fabric where giggles can fly.
Stitches of laughter in a cosmic quilt,
A patchwork of dreams that sunbeams have spilt.

Crafted together with swirls and sways,
Binding the moments in curious ways.
Snaps and pops from the creative spree,
As stars thread together, a comedy.

When the universe chuckles, all life reflects,
It's a humor made bright by celestial effects.
With stars as our guides, let's twirl and weave,
In this ludicrous dance, we'll always believe!

The Glow of Dawn's Promise

Morning arrives with a giggly stretch,
Sunbeams burst forth, no need to fetch.
With toast in the air and coffee in hand,
The dawn greets the day with a cheeky stand.

Birds chime in with their morning tunes,
A symphony bright, now who needs balloons?
As sunlight unrolls its golden reel,
The world's having fun with a radiant feel.

Clouds play hopscotch across the sky,
Chasing the shadows that flit on by.
A playful parade, a whimsical spin,
In the glow of the morn, let the giggles begin!

A Canvas of Stars

A splash of twinkle on the night's dark hue,
Spraying stardust like an artist would do.
Each spark a tickle, a giggle unleashed,
Painting the cosmos, a bright, silly feast.

Comets shoot by with a wink and a flip,
Hitchhikers of joy on a stellar road trip.
The universe chuckles as colors collide,
In this wild masterpiece, there's nowhere to hide.

From the canvas above, laughter pours down,
A jester's parade wearing sparkly gowns.
With laughter ignited, let's frolic and play,
In this cosmic carnival, we'll never stray!

Mosaics of Brightness

In the corner, a cat plays,
Chasing sunbeams, in a daze.
Paw prints on the window pane,
Little shadows, what a game!

A spilled drink on the floor,
Splashes of color, oh, what a chore!
Friends laugh as they slip and slide,
Joy dances where chaos can't hide.

Behold, the fridge's light gleams,
A midnight snack, oh, the schemes!
Glimmers in the dark like stars,
Food run wild behind Mars bars.

In the mix of chaos and cheer,
Life's hues appear, crystal clear.
Each silly moment, a radiant sight,
Mosaics of value, shining bright.

Gossamer Glints

A flying pie, a twist of fate,
Lands on a head, oh what a state!
Laughter erupts, it's quite the scene,
Who knew desserts could cause such a glean?

Balloons bobbing high with ease,
Squeaking gently in the breeze.
A dance of color, joyous delight,
Like confetti on a summer night!

Chasing fireflies without a clue,
They blink and tease, in shades of blue.
Falling down, we laugh till we cry,
Even starlight wants to fly!

Whispers of giggles and warming rays,
Wrap around us, brightening our days.
In every giggle and flinch of fate,
Life glimmers, a whimsical state!

Lattice of Illumination

A squirrel in shades, oh what a sight,
Stealing nuts and joy, pure delight.
His little dance, a comical show,
Sways and twirls, like he's stole the glow!

Lights on the eaves, sparking fun,
Chasing his tail, he says he won!
A burst of laughter, a playful chase,
Furry antics, such a funny race.

The neighbors join with lanterns bright,
Bumping elbows, a silly sight.
Each giggle threads through the night air,
Creating a quilt, of joy to share.

Together we laugh in sweet display,
Each moment, a spark, a zig-zag sway.
In the web of mirth, we share delight,
Creating warmth in the crisp moonlight.

Fragments of Daydream

A hammock's sway in the sunny glade,
Where every thought, like lemonade,
Zips and zags, like a playful breeze,
Drifting by, putting minds at ease.

Rain on the roof, a silly tune,
Sounds like laughter, a playful rune.
Dancing puddles sing along,
A symphony of giggles, not too long!

Jumping frogs in a jovial spat,
Chasing each other, imagine that!
They leap through puddles, a merry spree,
Jumping with joy, just like you and me.

In fragments of smiles, the day gleams bright,
Filling our hearts with sheer delight.
Silly moments weave through the air,
Capturing laughter, life's funny affair!

www.ingramcontent.com/pod-product-compliance
Lightning Source LLC
Chambersburg PA
CBHW060135230426
43661CB00003B/427